I0895647

THE ACQUIESCENT VILLA

THE ACQUIESCENT VILLA

POEMS

PAULA CLOSSON BUCK

LOUISIANA STATE UNIVERSITY PRESS
Baton Rouge
1998

Copyright © 1988, 1990, 1991, 1992, 1993, 1995, 1996, 1998, by Paula Closson Buck
All rights reserved
Manufactured in the United States of America
First printing
07 06 05 04 03 02 01 00 99 98 5 4 3 2 1

Designer: Laura Roubique Gleason
Typeface: Bembo with Serlio display
Printer and binder: Edwards Brothers, Inc.

Library of Congress Cataloging-in Publication Data

Buck, Paula Closson, 1957–
The acquiescent villa : poems / Paula Closson Buck.
p. cm.
ISBN 0-8071-2304-8 (alk. paper). — ISBN 0-8071-2305-6 (pbk.: alk. paper)
I. Title.
PS3552.U3339A65 1998
811'.54—dc21 98-27668
CIP

The author offers grateful acknowledgment to the editors of the following journals, in which some of the poems herein first appeared: *Antioch Reveiw:* "The Acquiescent Villa"; *Denver Quarterly:* "A Betrayal of Integers," "Off Season," "Room with Open Blinds"; *Ohio Review:* "After Childbirth," "The Balcony," "Discourse on Monogamy and Flight," "Star Chart Over the Bed," "The Road to Châteauneuf"; *Plum Review:* "Elegy," "The Turkish Baths"; *Shenandoah:* "Little Spanish Poems"; *Westminster Review:* "Berlin Correlative," "The Epithalamion of Piero Ridolfi"; *Willow Springs:* "From a Porthole," "The Man at Pensione Marta Looks at His Eye."

Thanks also go to the Virginia Center for the Creative Arts for supporting the author's period of residency there, during which she worked on this book.

The paper in this book meets the guidelines for permanence and durability of the Committee on Production Guidelines for Book Longevity of the Council on Library Resources. ♾

For Jim

CONTENTS

THE ACQUIESCENT VILLA

STAR CHART OVER THE BED

Beneath it he turns me, like an ocean a steamer
somewhere off Cyprus. In a storm
the body abandons its colors,
a sailor dropping hastily into the sea.

There is a world bigger than affection
or faithlessness, the mire Rimbaud sank in finally,
his legs swollen like amphitheaters,
the will to play the part long gone.

A whole nation of a man exhausts itself
in a single trail like a line of ink
laboring over a page. And the cities he might have been,
steamy at night, the countrysides of poppy

and the railyards where the soul
freights itself with passion are only paper,
the local need choosing for him
four o'clock and a greased, hungry sky.

At the screen door I stand,
sailing the rivulets the rain has made
in the gravel of the drive, my boat
too small for words.

FROM A PORTHOLE

We have snapshots of you
looking out at me looking out.

Birds were diving, bringing up fish.
But dying is different. The moon

capsized in a tree, the night's hull
rests high out of water.

And when you are afraid,
your features no longer

contain your face.
You choose a bright shirt to cover me.

You try to carry the moon in a bowl
while loud like a tourist

my blood brightens the sheet.
Los huevos son terrible I shout

and ride away on the body's
small train. The day we left Córdoba,

tired from fighting,
all the cars were shifting to one side.

I have loved one man. I've had a child
for one week, but in birth his shoulders

broke me. What can make him safe
when maybe for the last time

he has curled at my midriff—
one eye hidden,

one staring out
like an insect—alive six days.

AFTER CHILDBIRTH

Against azalea and forsythia's

shy arrival, a backhoe groans.
A doctor scribbles,
makes wind tearing paper. He scribbles as he might

spit seeds or as God
makes the first blobs of a spring rain.
Dyspareunia. Purply-black shrub of a word

that withers slowly when you carry it
out into the heat.
Even the ground is healing badly this spring,

full of ruts and broken.
At the family picnic
there is one great aunt who tints her hair red,

there is one with a bulldog's face.
The men who have come
from beneath their dresses have been to divinity school.

Still like boys
they peer up under the mind's
low hem. You might denounce your family

to join the immaculate order
of secrets men keep.
You might live inside like a monk, come out into Rome only

for bread and calamari
on your bicycle.
The oily squids in your basket, your soul

collates the sky, its leaves,
the air hammer, the genitalia
of fountains traduced in water. If this is a lie

at least it is your own.
Each night of your life
you have lain awake in sleep's narrow bed

listening for the dark
beyond the city
where the bears put on their masks with snouts,

where the one-legged women undress,
where your parents held each other
beside the Frigidaire. In the morning there was a starling

dead under the pear tree,
there was one among rotting pears
pushing its needle through the slick ground-leaves.

VIA DEL AMORE

The ivory lyrics of the sea are other
bodies swimming, flamboyant
and comfortable. Their suits
seed the rock like a pomegranate.

On these cliffs
as on a pair of high shoes
I am made formal. Far from water
I wear my arms like disability.

Here I have lived, talking to you
as though I must journey
from my vertiginous houses and my mouth
were a steep path words fumbled down.

I am not a shape
seen from a distance. I am the train's
stammering between two tunnels,
the wind tattered by the heat,

and it floats in irremediable scraps.
Don't look back at me, my love.
Below see the rock like a bull's side,
the tiny flags it wears of defeat and obstinacy.

THE EPITHALAMION OF PIERO RIDOLFI

After a short night's plumage of dreams
my love sleeps late, alone in her room.

November is ambivalent, and the Ginkgo leaves,
downed by wind, grow somber in golden pools.

I cannot know her, except as the sculptor
knows his stone the hour he cuts it.

And he washes his hands in the back room
of its beauty. At the table of the Medici

Buonarroti sits, stuffed on sweetmeats
and hens. Even now, he understands

that the Pope must die, that the world of means
is an unfinished cathedral.

Come to me, love, where the sky is remiss.
Come in the infirmity of caresses

to the vault of my ribs, this disappointed
heaven. At night the river is squid-ink black.

My mind ventures over, tense in its regalia.
Barges move, perpetual down the aisles of the dark.

I turn back the snow's wet veil. The gates are open,
but the people are leaving the city.

I attend pearl buttons like shore lights.
The works of the masters are burning in the street.

LITTLE SPANISH POEMS

I

Christ, from before this plate of figs
in the corpulent heat

I travel to you
as to a town in the distance.

There is a convent with iron crosses,
a plaza with cedars, and a woman

who's washed my sense
white on a long-handled brush.

The sun, slipped down the sky,
leaves a gold ring

the day moves
back and forth on its finger.

II

I read of a freighter trawling
the sea for years and a place to dump.

Winter of carbolic moons.
Grimy palms and daylight.

So I tried to sleep
last night but all the ports were closed.

I walked an interior as broad
and coarse as the face of a Turk.

And high above the streets I listened for
their synchronous clapping.

III

After the fight and the blood of the bull,
after the hot-tempered dust

and the sherry, he chases her
around a sapling in the courtyard,

wanting to scare up some cry
to confuse with delight. Above, the sun

is a wheel on an axle;
below, the broken car of its passage.

We went away once to the sea,
you and I; we watched the strait

for a ship. But our luggage was stolen
in the street in Cádiz. There's a light

in the eyes of the old fascists,
there's a history smudged out in the heart.

IV

I lie sometimes wasted in sleep like two grains
I rub between my thumb and my forefinger.

In that rest, my feet are a platitude,
my arms divorced. The men come out

from their villages bearing the dead.
Nearby they hawk silks for favors.

I am too weak to buy, too weak to resume
the pallet of my going. There's a hawk

that floats above me. There is one with the road
on its wings. I am driving

from blank to blank and cannot remember
what happiness wracked me when I set out.

THE ROAD TO CHÂTEAUNEUF

Tall and spare as an elm you went down,
your anger listing in the final breeze,

bitter eyes gone to ubiquity, like crickets
working their destructions on the night.

A woman searches the house, lifting rugs,
crawls from room to room of devoured silence.

We walk her solitude.
The grapes still green, we walk the thirst of stones,

when out from your heart climbs the sun
on broken feet, and the day we haul like an ingot,

brilliant and heavy, toward town.
Hours gather, and men at a fountain.

Overhead, pigeons circle and shift,
circle and shift to exhaust our watching.

Who is the leader?
Whose idea to turn back this time?

AWAKE

I lie in my bed fully clothed, some guilt
rendering me conscious. Far away, Somalian guerillas

drink baby formula in the dust.
I see them wipe the thick, sweet milk

from their three-days' growth.
They are lanky, at rest from violence.

It is geography that lets me love
the man beside me now, and time

trimming its nails in the lamplight.
Once he was the boy I never knew.

In a house in Dayton, he lay
with his head propped in his mother's hand,

hair threshed back beneath a warm faucet.
How many years later I have crossed

the desert of him, humped like a dromedary.
Between the child's face waiting and the eye

that finally sleeps, whole cultures must be lost,
cargoes raided, neon put out.

A small boy stands at the sink washing dishes,
his sleeves pushed up past the elbow,
his little belly sopping up spills.

In the attic above him, wasps
nest beneath a shade.
He has been told they will be taken out

before they awake in springtime.
Will you let the birds out? he asks.
I don't know how

since he thinks of them as birds,
though tiny, unseen.
When the morning haze crept

like baby sight through the blinds
on this first warm day
he must have awakened

thinking of them. Now his hand
travels to the faucet again,
a colony of bubbles alive on his fist.

Once all touching was oblique
as if here were the word
jasmine, there the nameless flowers.

Now that this man
has looked me in the face and kept on looking
past the moment

of shudder and refrain,
words and their stuff
yawn before me

in a house where the sky
hangs in squares.
But when he looks at me

from the side, like that, like a Picasso—
one eye on a plane of the face
peering over—he is tailing my descent,

as if down the last
cathedral's serpentine step,
his ten-gallon teeth

laughing in the dark
behind me, the chinchilla happiness
of his chest stuffed

beneath a stone shirt.
Outside, the trees move
like waiters at a darkened café.

It has been raining,
but only locally.
I have not told the truth yet.

THE MAN AT PENSIONE MARTA LOOKS AT HIS EYE

He squints as the portrait
                                        clouds, greenish
gray, gray like the sea outside
his window, he advances
                                        and recedes, a subtle untruth
before himself. How long has he traveled
this dissimulation and how long sat
                                                    in the margin

waving a white hanky

while dusk and its eyeful of swallows refused
to render him? Fixing again
the rubber-banded frames
                                        above his ears, he floats
into the garden, his senses weeding
                                                    him from roses.

THE BALCONY

after Manet

Hurricane beauty fixed by a paper fan,
dark hair poised about her face,
she looks out from the balcony,
proprietor of dissatisfaction.

In the distant afternoon, poplars
waver with smoke from a factory.
When she walked there once,
the briars stung her hand and crimson

beads decorated her skin
as sweat does a porcelain pitcher, or sadness now
her fine white dress.

Sometimes I wish I could fly away,
hasten the lethargic air and leave
others to lie
behind sane faces. The heart's red dahlias

grapple with the rain. If love were a storm
and this the quiet following,
she'd have stood out under the electric
trees for hours and not turned home.

THE TURKISH BATHS

Like those who plotted freedom in the fifties
from these greenish basins, I too have drifted
beyond an hour, and water has spumed from the mouths

of ornate fish into mine.
I have dwelt forever in the municipality of breasts.
But outside I am again personal, like anyone

afraid a dream will come to nothing.
In Budapest I bet on the horses
but at random, to cheat bad logic.

When the numbers were hoisted down from the sky,
the afternoon still heaving and sweating,
the ground lay thick with stubs

like a provisional happiness.
All I've wanted was the nobility of which,
on an evening like this, the heart feels capable.

To belong to the lithography of place—
the city that exchanges white skylines across the river
against a leaded sky. But somewhere tonight

my horses lie down, truncated in the dark.
And after the competition of the hours
when I move toward sleep, I grow restlessly occupied

like the communists with their wheelbarrows
hurrying documents from the statehouse in Prague.
They know that time cannot promise them much

against these smallest hours. I look out
as if through the dirty window of a tram.
In cafés, the young are roused over newsprint,

drinking late. One needs to unlearn expectancy,
but they are all night
pissing and waiting in the embassy courtyards.

1989

CHANDELIERS FROM AN OLD REGIME

1.

In the heat his face is impassive.
A man eating boiled pork

at a roadside hall. Women and a boy
climb the spiral stair to a restroom.

Above the oak banister
and the woodwork's unimpeachable

captions, new portraits.
                                        Death is not
the mother of beauty.
The afternoon has drained its bowl

to soup bones and permanence,
square tables where people

know what to expect. As if
one arm did not hang quite right,

broken and healed
with no sling, their rest is conscious.

2.

Outside, the rain exposes
its high forehead. So much space

and a single idea. He wrote a letter.
He wrote another.
                    In the face of a guard
at the border he has seen youth

like a tract of night
glimpsed through the open window of a train.

East Germany, 1988

BERLIN CORRELATIVE

Over the shores of newsprint
Sophie Charlotte drifts in sleep
no one looks out
at the lit box
Rain and the malady of possession
where a guard presses his face
Sophie whispers Frederick
to the glass and is gone
Do you love me?
The station stands empty
dirt under the nails
of two cities
He loves her better

The chestnuts begin
dying from a standstill
With four straight-
no yellow or senile orange
backed chairs
I could live without fear
but death between thirty and forty
rope my hearing off
when summer says its name
and suffer only

through the milk teeth of the cold
the brief intent of tea roses

Frederick has built a palace
In the brain-
with fuchsias made to stand
like trees
gray evening headlights sweep
two warriors frozen at the gate
since life is short
half a city

1988

GEBURTSTAG / BIRTHDAY

The room is white
where I am sketched, a line

drawing, an example of my self.
I cannot furnish it.

Having taken into account the roses,
the *Collected Poems* of Paul Celan,

the delicate bowl, still I cast around.
In a city where no one works,

only the heavy sky procures me,
and the rook that picks up for flight

from my sudden chest to the copper eaves.
Thirty years across a bright façade

I weep an inclement green.
How long does weight take?

How fathomless is noon. Somnambulant
lines, will you die if I wake you?

MY MOTHER'S GARDEN

Already the finity of feeling provokes
its ritual of ants, like a rind.
Six o'clock is the pink's
defoliation. *Her round arm pale*
as the belly of a fish, the fair one glides the river in Chekhov.

The hour carps in the shallows
where eaves overhang rhubarb and columbine
(my mother creeping with her trowel).

What little has survived
the blunder: *gone*
the swimmer's clothes from the grassy bank.
When she is a woman
most, she has fled
to these palest hours when the sun gapes coxcomb
red, among perennials
amid the sumptuous vegetables.

THE ACQUIESCENT VILLA

Schubert is residual, Brahms
with the pedal sustaining. My mother
has canceled her picnic at Lake Michigan.

I will play a sonata with feeling,
my hands straying, like dogs over broken
tile and myrtle, clematis and beer-glass,

beneath the erratic phrasing of swallows.
Someone builds a villa on a premise:
swimming pool, terrace,

a balcony where guests will linger,
remarking Ursa Major on the sky.
But March comes like an argument,

April the bearing out of eventual distaste.
He is seen taking the phonograph and then,
alone in the scullery, in the open

salon, practice blows softly
at the neck of decline.
I keep playing as the rooms spring weeds,

B-natural in the key of F, I play stiff
arpeggios, trills like black pearls
nibbling at a collarbone.

What brings a house down?
Is it the keening of insects, the snails
blithering up deaf walls?

Am I the invention of this regress?
Like the gray toil of cloud and corruptible
orange at the sky's underlimit,

the fires in the olive grove
are spent in half an evening.
I am thirty, but time is not prepared

for the lingering of an instance.
While I play *Deux Arabesques,* while I belabor
the two-against-three and the trucks

haul their requiem of fumes uphill,
the Great Bear rides over—obtuse, serene,
unhinging my parlor from the universe.

ROOM WITH OPEN BLINDS

One wants to disappear these short nights
when everything's in place—table, bed—

the real a document: the world in its specificity
fails again. The sun's reduced

on venetian blinds to a glint.
The lights on in my room

bring the dark down.
In Spain, a Moorish cathedral boasts

striped columns, various in height,
a vestibule to the inconsistent.

The light in my room brings the dark
down against that gaudy retreat of the sun,

and the Bargello's crenellations, the Duomo's
pajama print. It fixes the quotidian

wish of house plants. Still, outside,
riding his bike, I can hear the boy Milton.

Someone has forgotten
to call him out of the absence.

THE ERRAND

Between departing and the loaf of bread,
between your door
                    and the plague of white moths the mini-mart suffered
last summer, you know the other man waits.
His shadow is patient among the hedgerows.

                                                            If you loved him, just a little,
you became a little grotesque, like the figures your husband
  sketches in coal,
their tiny heads spoiling the big, beautiful thumbs.
                                                                        Somehow, you too
have run afoul of beauty, though it was everywhere,
                    bringing you gifts.
And though your child's hair is silken
                                                            at nighttime to your touch,
you may never arrive at the well-lit stoop, paper bag in hand.
Evening's slow candor receives you again. From among

the day's artifacts, a geranium has plucked something red.
                                                In the scroll and smudge of dying light,
sustained like the humor of the bereft,

things hold their shapes.
                                            You are beginning to see the human face
as the only form of righteousness.

Forehead when the hair's smoothed back.
Carthusian meeting of nose
with upper lip. What remains
of stories and vows,
stacked below in the mouth's deep catacomb.

ELEGY

When I am naked, alone, when I have abdicated
my socks, my lips,

when your death has left me
obvious, a field mouse traveling

the belly of a snake, and I find myself
whole in the gulf of your absence,

there is no audience
and no betrothal, no rhyme but a shadow

from the light strung over the bed.
For all our exertions there is never

more than a dreamed-up
lover. By what short stem

were you attached to the ground?
You who believed in tall cedars like endings.

OFF SEASON

Who I am I lay out on these rocks
whole in my bad
disposition, unthreatened by the waves' idle

Schopenhauer, Schopenhauer.
Prolific and balding, a man

strolls in dark shorts near the water—
his wrinkles and rolls
scribbling away

to the cursive of plovers.
What do they write on a porcelain sky?

The mind of God is a room that receives me—

its clean towels like ministers,
its bidet a vase

for the loyalty of the thighs, and the belly as chaste
as a mum, and the deep black poppy.

PORNOGRAPHY

To make her want to make love
to him, across the arid expanse of her
ambivalence, he draws an Arab woman in a palanquin.
What's a palanquin? she asks.
                                        A conveyance,
he tells her. She listens and looks out,
as if through a slit in black cloth, at the world he projects.
Like a litter? she asks.
                                Synonyms are important
in this business, he tells her. This morning
she watched the neighbor's boxer
beat off at a garbage can
        in the rain. Its red member glistened,
pornographic. Like all the exposed world.
Cripples and reliefers gathered at the Tastee Creme
in noonday sunshine, their pink tongues lashing
at the fleeting mirage of taste.
                                        He is losing her
so she listens hard to his voice.
The old sharpei listens too, from the other side of the door.
Visible beneath, one yellow ear marks off
the rooms of habit, keeping the worn pages
        from the unthumbed stack.
                                    She is trying to find where she left off
but each paragraph reminds her, when it's done,

that she's been there before. From him, like a bone,
the days keep unearthing her.
                                        Had he bought her
with a goat in some provincial village
he'd have given up by now. One child
from her narrow hips, breasts contracted like bulbs
pulled and left on the walk.
                                        But he has paid nothing
and so she must awaken, like anyone capable of love.
Dunes of blond fur luff up from the hardwood floor.
        An American tourist lifts his wife's
culotte and rocks against her
in the Arab sand, their bodies hot in argument. His teeth
                graze her shoulder bone, pages flapping now
like pillowcases in a wind.
                                        The dog must have gone
to the kitchen for a drink. It is dry in the Arab town.
The tamped soil of the street barely speaking
beneath their heels reminds her of Durrell, but apocryphal,
noncirculating. How well he knows her.
                                        The rickety
gharry of his voice comes close then runs down
on the other side of the dark, where heat lightning
flashes its fitful eloquence
                over her body's eastern quarter.

On any evening in summer, she would leave
this life with him for the rarest fiction
his love can offer, the most tenuous
sentence he can speak her out of.

DISCOURSE ON MONOGAMY AND FLIGHT

1. Levels of Flight

The fly is immediate: its dirt-bike
motor and attachable lust,

its gasoline wings in the sun,
the legs that relish, in front

and behind. The bee,
promiscuous, works close by,

stem after stem in clover.
A spider glides tangentially

on a cord of hidden silk.
In the middle distance,

titmice and larks, then high up,
buzzards whelming the sky.

But the fly, unabashed, negotiates
the nubs of a shin like a husband,

lets off then resumes
with a petroliferous arm.

2. Disequilibrium

It is not so much the stranger
as misdirected desire for the lover

absent. *No* is as tenuous in the air
as a dinner bell. Where are the monks

who were to gather in your hips?
They are hot, they have gone in,

forsaking conversation.
You angle for words

to seize the air diminishing
between you. Words are listless.

Sitters on chairs, they ask you for water,
they want to sleep late. *To want.*

Infinitive. You wait for the train,
signals all flashing in tubular silence.

3. Earhart

At first she dug her toes into the sharp shells
of the beach, glad to be alive—even as the days

drifted past and nights condensed the shore
to a thin, bold headline. She knew it must read

NEAR-DEATH RELIEF FOR AVIATOR.
Only the tacked-on heel of a shoe

identifies her decades later, her plane
having washed out in a storm. In the end,

she is matched with the paraphernalia of a life,
though she fell fully out of her name,

radio waves crackling while anonymous
she made smoke on desert islands.

4. Equilibrium

For all the wheat brushed onto these hills,
for the green motive of trees and the train that stuns

the evening air, there is room. For the cow
walking near, her coat a meteor shower,

her head abject in moonlight. I don't know how
to find you in the domesticity of feet, how not

to touch you with hands as dark and light
as beetles, used to a little death for sustenance.

In the curved space of the night,
in time that slackens as we rest against it,

low-beams slur us where we sit, not
cows, not lovers, not broken by need.

5. For a Bat Hung Upside Down in Daylight

There is no reason for this
bat's hunger, but his tiny

mouth falls open, kissed with flies.
As he allows day to find

him so, I let night happen
sometimes, the mistake

of darkness spilling across
me where I lie in my dress.

When I married, I wore bat wing
sleeves of lace, my hair snarled up

in a bat's paradise. I don't
remember the death perfume

that I inhale now, courtesy
of the heat and one who hangs

open mouthed where I've
left her, exposed on sleep's barb.

6. Holiday for One

Delphi

Despite the rocky innuendo of the ground,
the cypress stands, a syllable

the sky has pronounced
without moving its pale mouth.

It would be Gogol's idea
of a holiday for one.

Only you can read its seismographic
sadness. Good-bye to the beautiful

stranger who claimed he was your double.
Good-bye to the monk with a face

like gravity, far above the sea.
Here is the liturgy of a barbarous calm,

green and dense as a fly's tail:
Sky crater. Soul cone.

A BETRAYAL OF INTEGERS

Cumberland Island, Georgia

We have counted ninety egrets swooning
into the trees behind the mansion
where the Carnegies used to hang
their white towels. Birds, towels:
intelligible sums, like oranges and oranges.
Subtract from them the sea

and the sea turtle transmogrified
on the strand. The buzzards' code has settled to a pine tonight
though the blue dark is still
as distant as the cold
that entered a room on a woman's shawl.

When she walked among the peregrine fronds,
and seed ticks
found the pale inversions of her knees,
from where did she return
to disturb the immense
polygons of evening, opening a line, trailing
bits of wet
leaf across an oriental rug?

HUSBAND IN THE TREES

Over the plane of dark
                                        trunks white stones
between us, I am moving toward you slantwise,

out of our small apartment
                                        like a bishop muttering
the names of peace. The sun has progressed;

the sky is a continent.
                                        I know you sit in the cemetery trees, eating
a laborer's lunch. But you do not know my wandering

among coppered mausoleums
                                        where the larger mysteries
grow scrutible. The angels are obvious, sentimental,

like white sand beaches
                                        the bathers have left,
affairs become wives. In the seascaped cities where I thought

I knew you best
                                        even the postcard blondes were dated.
You bought them in a hurry to spend your last *lire.*

Before the train I saw you
as if far away with your paper bag,
distorted, prepared to embrace the future like an outgrown

past. The doors close and close.
To love is to choose
to love anonymously the familiar, openly the strange.

I am reading cards over
your shoulder at noon. I'm attempting
a transfer of pawns, the way I've persuaded you

to trade sides of the bed
so I'd sleep in your rest
and then endure long weeks when mine was mine

and yours still becoming
more slowly, enigmatically
yours. How strange will I seem to you

here on the ground
with my tiny family
of schoolgirls who've gathered to point and to marvel?

In Rome, where the Pope
                    loomed bigger than life
over the Vatican on postcards—the triumph of faith

an aesthetic failure—
                    only the diesel snore of busses
penetrated the dark in our room. I watched while you slept

and in your eyelids
                    and nose saw the incorruptible
no that is occasion for our mouths when we're lovers.

THIN WOMAN AT THE OPERA

From my cheap seat in the dark
I can barely see
Pavarotti, immense on stage in his posh cloak.

And I cannot see his chest
heave under the spot
though I understand why he must sing and love

and grieve while standing
perfectly still. Behind the wheel
of the soul's inebriate ride, the body apologizes

for everything bigger than life—
extravagant eyes, false identities.
For the dim poison of touch, like carp rising in fulvous water.

The Christian women next door
double over
to think they might confess affairs, or love

that won't bear keeping.
Through the bathroom window screen,
I hear their hazel voices, sure of what they are,

then silence, like that
                                        of a smoker exhaling. At the back of my house,
my small son claps a few times in the dark.

He is not immune to joy,
                                                        sporadic and emptying
through the hands. And when the quiet like a lung breathes us

out onto our pillows,
                                                I might be gone to where I am
no longer complicit in injury or pardon.

Though I am his mother.
                                                        When night falls
I bring the windows down. If life is as small as a house,

it is shaped like the aria's drift
                                                                easing into rooms
two lovers have lived in comfortably, while a third, like a mole,

opened passage underground.
                                                                Though I have sent him away,
the yard sinks beneath the weight of my foot. At night

what I know is rendered in stillness.
Through a door left ajar,
my son looks in wonder, as if I'd emerged

whole from the sea,
one leg poised on the toilet's shell,
the other, monolithic, rising from blue-green tile.